An INCONVENIENT Christmas

Joseph S. Bonsall

Illustrated by Jonathan Taylor

New Leaf Press

First printing: August 2004
Second printing: October 2008

Illustrated by Jonathan Taylor,
www.jonathantaylorart.com
Interior design by Bryan Miller

Based on the song, "The Most Inconvenient Christmas," written by Kyle Matthews
(BMG Songs, Inc./See For Yourself Music, copyright 2000)
and recorded by the Oak Ridge Boys on Spring Hill Music.

ISBN: 0-89221-590-9
Library of Congress Catalog Card Number: 2004109635

Printed in United States of America

Please visit our website for more great titles:
www.newleafpress.net

New Leaf Press

To my wonderful grandchildren,
Breanne and Luke

Foreword

Frances and I have been honored to be associated with Joe and the rest of the Oak Ridge Boys for several decades! Their dedication and energy have been used, time and time again, to help Feed the Children. Many hungry kids across the United States of America — and around the world — have had food to eat because of our joint efforts. From food drops to television specials and promotional events, the Oaks, like so many others, have given their love and support to Feed the Children. We will always be grateful.

I came to know Joe as an author through a touching book about his parents, *G.I. Joe and Lillie*. So I was honored that he asked me to write the foreword for this special story, *An Inconvenient Christmas*. In it, Joe takes Kyle Matthews's song, which was made popular by the Oaks, and brings it to life by creating the Winsteads, an all-American family with whom we can all identify!

The Winsteads' story is so perfectly relevant in our fast-paced world today! And in this wonderful Christian family book, Joe sprinkles the message with a mix of humor and expediency. By the end of the tale, the Winsteads have experienced a life-changing lesson. They have come to better understand the very first Christmas, when God sent His only Son to be born of a virgin in a manger. They have learned the true meaning of Christmas — and that the most inconvenient Christmas in history was the first one! It's a humbling and inspiring revelation!

Many times during the hustle and bustle of our own Christmas season, we get so wrapped up in putting up the decorations, buying presents, preparing for family, and cooking a good meal that we forget those less fortunate. There are many children who have nothing to eat and little to celebrate. Our mission at Feed the Children is to remember them, at Christmas as well the rest of the year.

As we celebrate this blessed season, please pray for these children, and if you feel led, give us a call at 1-888-435-7382 (1-888-HELPFTC) to make a donation. Your call can help us send out another Feed the Children truck full of food. It only happens with your help!

Thanks, Joe, for a terrific story. Thanks, Kyle, for a wonderful song. And thank you, Oak Ridge Boys, for your friendship.

God bless you all! I hope you enjoy this inspiring book! Merry Christmas!

—Larry Jones
President of Feed the Children

Author's notes

This book started with a song! A few short years ago, Oaks' lead singer and song man Duane Allen was searching for material for our Spring Hill Christmas project. He came across an incredible little tune called "The Most Inconvenient Christmas," written by cutting edge, contemporary Christian songwriter, Kyle Matthews.

We had recorded one of Kyle's great songs, "Fall To Fly," on our *From the Heart* Gospel project, and we were very familiar with his style. But this song was really different. What a piece of work! A great story with a tremendous message that was woven into an incredible melody and chord structure — very Kyle Matthews!

We loved the song, and it quickly became the flagship song for the project. In fact, we called the CD *An Inconvenient Christmas* and named our Christmas tour and our Feed the Children television special the same.

The song was now a part of our lives. The author side of me believed that the subject could also make for a great Christian family book, so I created the Winsteads to live out the basic story of the song – with a lot of artistic embellishment along the way. What fun! What a blessing!

I want to thank Tim Dudley and all of my friends at New Leaf Press for believing in this book and for putting it in your hands.

I thank Kathy Harris and Gary Spicer for their hard work and friendship.

I thank my Mary Ann for her love and constant support in all that I do.

Thanks to my singing partners, Duane Allen, William Lee Golden, and Richard Sterban for always being there beside me with love and friendship.

I really appreciate Rev. Larry Jones of Feed the Children for taking the time to write the foreword for this book. Our long-time friend always brings a keen perspective as it relates to the wonderful work that he and his lovely wife, Frances, do for hungry children everywhere. What an honor to have him take part!

I thank Jonathan Taylor for the tremendous illustrations and for bringing the Winsteads to life.

I thank my friend Celeste Winstead at Spring Hill Music, Inc. for allowing me to use her very cool name. (She thanked me for giving her a husband!)

I want to thank Kyle Matthews for the huge part that he plays in this project. I have a lot of love and respect for him! He is not only a great singer and writer, but he is a well-known Christian speaker who is leading a lot of kids to Christ. Visit him online at www.kylematthews.com.

Most of all I want to thank our Lord and Savior Jesus Christ for leaving heaven on that very first "inconvenient Christmas" long ago, so that someday He would die on a wooden Cross for me . . . and for you. When our journey here on Earth is over, we will see Him and rejoice in His love. This is the real promise of what Christmas is all about!

God bless you, reader. I hope this little story is a blessing to your home and family. See you out there on the road!

– Joseph S. Bonsall

5

An Inconvenient Christmas

The Winsteads were preparing for a trip to Grandpa's house. It was early in the afternoon of Christmas Eve, and Celeste was packing up a few snacks and such for the trip to the country, while her husband James urged the two kids to hurry on up a bit. The day had really gotten away from them and they were leaving much later than originally planned.

"We are burning daylight here. Let's go, slow pokes," he yelled from the bottom of the stairs just hoping that he was being listened to. Any attempt at a positive response would be welcome.

"Coming, Dad!" came the positive response from seven-year-old Melissa.

"What about your brother?" James asked.

"He is being a turkey," laughed the beautiful raven-haired little girl. "But I think he is almost ready."

"Gobble, gobble!" laughed the voice of Melissa's eleven-year-old brother, Sam. The boy was in his bedroom that was also known as NASCAR Head-quarters. The sign that hung on the outside of his usually closed door simply read, "PIT AREA — KEEP OUT!"

7

"I'm comin', Dad," Sam replied from deep within the "pit area."

Melissa and Sam Winstead were really excited about seeing old Grandpa Luke. He lived on a farm about two hours out of town. The ride was kind of boring, but seeing ol' Lucas (as their father called him) was always well worth the trip. Besides, he may even have some cool presents this year, but that was doubtful. Grandpa just didn't leave the farm very often since Grandma Emma passed away a few years ago.

"Honey, would you go outside and get the mail?" asked Celeste. "I think it's been in the mailbox for a couple of days now."

James put on his favorite down jacket which was "really toasty" and walked down the driveway toward the mailbox. The ground felt all crunchy from the morning frost.

The Winsteads lived in a beautiful little subdivision outside of the big city called Sandy Cove (although there wasn't any sand or even a cove to be found anywhere). The houses here were very nice and very affordable as well. The two-story, red brick home with the quaint little backyard and decent-sized front lawn looked a bit like all the others around it, however the Winsteads were really quite happy here. The schools were good and the neighborhood seemed safe. The mall wasn't too far away and the neighbors were nice. James was a very successful accountant and business was pretty good these days. James Winstead thought that life was good and at Christmas time, life was *great*!

He walked by the plastic Santa Claus and reindeer that adorned his now icy lawn and stopped for a moment to adjust Rudolph. He wasn't pointing in quite the right direction. "There now, that's better," thought James as he whistled a chorus of the red-nosed reindeer song.

James brought the mail in through the garage door that led to the kitchen and placed the small stack of mostly catalogs on the counter. The kids ran by in a colorful splash of bright outerwear.

"Button up, kids; it's really cold. There's frost on the old pumpkin this morning," he said as he kissed his wife on the cheek. "Love you, Honey!"

"I love you, too, James. Merry Christmas. Thanks for taking us to see Dad today. He gets really lonely out there on that farm since Mama died," Celeste whispered.

"Hey now," cooed James. "It's always nice to see him. I love that old man as much as you do."

The Winsteads had formulated a plan. They figured they would drive out to see Grandpa, have dinner with him at the farm and return home in time to get the kids off to bed early enough so as not to interfere with the arrival of Santa Claus. Then, tomorrow, just the four of them would enjoy Christmas morning together.

They would gather around the Christmas tree in the living room, open presents, shoot home movies, and listen to Christmas music on the stereo. Then, they would eat a nice turkey dinner with all the fixin's.

Later on, some friends would arrive. The kids would play with their new toys and the adults would laugh and tell stories of Christmases past while watching football on television. There would be snacks and smiles and a good time would be had by all on this festive Yuletide day.

Oh, what a storybook time. Middle America at its very best, except for the fact that the Winsteads were about to come face-to-face with a very inconvenient Christmas. Absolutely *nothing* would go as planned.

It all started to go downhill with the reading of the mail. James was carrying some things out to the family Jeep Cherokee when Celeste called out to him.

"You have a problem here with Shopazon-dot-com," she yelled from the kitchen.

"What? How could that be?" replied James as he entered the kitchen and picked up the dreaded letter that his wife handed over for him to read.

The message was very clear and to the point. "The Christmas gifts you ordered aren't in stock. They have been placed on backorder and will arrive on January 15 unless you cancel this order by December 24. Thank you for shopping online at SHOPA-ZON.COM and have a MERRY CHRISTMAS!"

"Huh?" cried James. "Didn't Charlie, the UPS guy, deliver these packages the other day?"

"I don't think so, Hon," answered Celeste as she rifled through her catalogs.

"I saw four big boxes on the front step three days ago. I assumed that they were from Shopazon," James said as his stomach began to churn. "I figured that I would wrap them up tonight."

"Oh, no, they were my orders from Spiegel," replied Celeste.

"But those boxes were huge! Are you sure?" James asked, although he already knew the answer.

"My stuff, Hon," exclaimed Celeste with a sad tone in her voice. "New sheets and a bedspread and pillow shams for the holidays. No Shopazon. Sorry."

"Oh man. The one year that I buy all my gifts on

that darn computer and this happens!" James was almost in tears. He had purchased a necklace and a set of earrings for Celeste. A complete Christmas Barbie set which included five outfits for Melissa, and a Michael Waltrip jacket, as well as a model of Michael Waltrip's NASCAR racecar for Sammy. He had also ordered a new Sony Playstation 2 with games for each of them, including a "John Madden Football" game for himself. Also, now on backorder were several DVDs and a new cutting-edge digital DVD player for the entire family.

I was going to be a hero and now I am going to be a goat, thought James. *Perhaps Wal-Mart or something will be open late tonight and we can stop there on the way home from Grandpa Luke's. Yeah! That's the ticket!* The thought made him feel a little better, but not much!

Celeste interrupted from inside the Cherokee. "James, let's go! We are burning daylight here."

Sam and Melissa were laughing from the backseat.

"Come on, Dad!" yelled Melissa.

"While we are still young," laughed Sam, utilizing one of his dad's favorite expressions.

James Winstead climbed behind the wheel and proceeded to back out of the garage. He made his usual move left and drove on out of the driveway. Once outside of Sandy Cove he turned north on County Route 52 and headed the Cherokee toward Grandpa's farm. James sat grim faced and quiet as he drove.

He was still mad at pretty much the entire Internet. The kids argued loudly in the backseat as to whether or not cows faced the same direction on purpose and Celeste just stared out the window watching the frosty countryside of her own childhood fly by the window. *I have to get that turkey in the oven around 4 a.m.,* she thought. Then she looked up at the sky and turned toward her husband. "Looks like a snow storm coming, Hon. The sky is getting really dark!"

James grunted!

The blizzard hit without warning — a regular whiteout. James could hardly make out the road in front of him. The snow was falling fast and hard at a fierce angle right toward the windshield. He slowed the SUV down as much as he could. He still had to maintain a little speed so that no one would crash into his backside. Bright lights didn't work at all. They just reflected back in his face and made things worse, so James had to be content with his lights on dim and the fog lights.

"Oh, wow! It's like the North Pole, Dad," said Sam.

"Don't hit Rudolph!" cried Melissa.

"You kids be quiet so Daddy can concentrate on his driving," said Celeste who was more than a little concerned.

Then she noticed something that looked like smoke rising from the hood.

"What is that, James?" she asked.

"Nothing, Celeste," answered James. "Just the snow melting on the hot hood."

"Oh. What does the temperature gauge say?"

James looked down at the dashboard. *Women!* he thought.

"Ahhhhhhhhhhh, the thing is locked on red! The engine is about to blow!"

James could barely make out the sign ahead through the blanket of falling snow.

Bub's Garage
Your Town Truck Stop
Food, Fuel, Service
Come on in!

He remembered the place. *Thank God,* he thought as he slowly pulled into the icy driveway of Your Town Truck Stop. He drove the smoking Jeep Cherokee up to a closed garage door and beeped the horn.

14

"Turn it off!" yelled a man dressed out in a pair of Blue Carhartt coveralls. "*Off!*"

His white nametag that was stitched just above his heart simply read, "Bub."

At Bub's command, James immediately switched off the engine. Now, the only discernible sound was a loud and steady hiss that erupted from deep beneath the hood of the Cherokee.

"James Winstead has pulled into Pit Row," announced Samuel from the backseat in his best NASCAR voice. "That car is in a heap of trouble, race fans!"

James, Celeste, and Melissa just couldn't help laughing out loud at Sammy. Besides, what more could go wrong on this "happy" Christmas Eve?

James got out and raised the hood and Bub started investigating.

Celeste told the kids to stay right there with Daddy and proceeded to walk through a side door that led her into the restaurant and convenience store section of the truck stop. She had seen a sign that read "Homemade Christmas Eggnog" as they pulled in. There were only a few folks in the entire place and a red-haired girl named Margie filled her order of five eggnogs. After a "Merry Christmas," a good tip, and a wave, Celeste headed back out front where she found Bub holding something in his hand. It looked somewhat like a dead snake.

With a dark expression on their faces, the kids and James were all peering at the fried piece of rubber in Bub's hands.

Bub was speaking in a hushed and seemingly reverent tone of voice as Celeste passed out Styrofoam cups full of hot, truck stop eggnog to each of them.

"You know those commercials on TV where they tell you that your heart is just fine . . . until it isn't? Well, it's the same with a fan belt," said Bub.

The five of them just stood there sipping eggnog on this snowy and stormy Christmas Eve.

"Good news is, the engine is just fine," exclaimed Bub, as he sipped his eggnog and smiled at Celeste.

"Is it too stupid of me to think that perhaps, by chance, just maybe, you might have a fan belt in stock that will fit this thing?" asked James as he pointed to the wounded Jeep.

"What year is this here Cherokee?"

"2001!"

"Nope." said Bub. He then did an abrupt about-face, took a few steps and walked through a side door and disappeared inside. James just shrugged his shoulders and looked at his wife.

"We can call Ken and Jane Dye, Honey," whispered Celeste. "They can come and get us."

"I hate to bother our neighbors this late on Christmas Eve, Hon," exclaimed James although he realized that there just might not be any real choice in the matter. He handed Celeste his cell phone. "Oh well, call em' up then."

"What about Grandpa, Daddy?" asked Melissa.

"Better call Lucas as well, Celeste."

Just then, Bub came back out with what looked suspiciously like a fan belt dangling out of his greasy right hand.

"My Cherokee is a '99 model. This should work," said Bub as he went back under the still upraised hood of the wounded Winstead SUV.

"Yes!" yelled Sam. "The pit boss comes through for James Winstead. He can't win this race, ladies and gentleman, but he can sure pick up a few points by just getting that car back on the track."

Melissa laughed out loud. Her big brother was so funny.

"Thanks, Bub," said Celeste. "Is that your real name? And how are you going to get home?"

"Not a problem, ma'am. My wife, Margie, will take me home in the pickup. My name is Dave. Dave Boots. My poppa named me Bub when I was little. You folks will be on your way in just a few more minutes."

"Thanks, Dave," said James Winstead, extending his hand. "This was sure nice of you. Merry Christmas to you and Margie."

"Well, that is what Christmas is all about, isn't it? Hey, I'm just glad that I could help. My Margie made this here eggnog we've been drinking."

There were handshakes and hugs all around.

Within ten minutes, the Winsteads were back on the road heading for Grandpa Luke's farm. It was a lot later than originally planned, but they were on their way.

"Did you call Lucas?" asked James.

"I tried," answered Celeste, "but I couldn't get through. Must have been the storm."

The weather began to clear as the family drove on through the evening. It was still really cold but, at least, the snow had stopped and thanks to Dave and Margie Boots, all seemed well. The fan belt was working and the eggnog had hit the spot. James began to smile as he drove.

All smiles and good feelings evaporated as James pulled into Grandpa Luke's long and winding driveway. There were fire engines and police cars and all sorts of emergency vehicles parked all around what was once a beautiful two-story white bungalow-type farmhouse. The whirling red and blue lights were reflecting off the smoldering remains. The acrid mell of smoke was everywhere as James, Celeste, and the two kids threw open the car doors and started running toward the mess. A huge fire hose and pump were sticking out of the pond by the house and James tripped over the hose and, in so doing, did a nifty face plant into the frozen mud between the

pond and the barn. No one even noticed.

"Dad!" screamed Celeste as she nimbly stepped over the hose in full stride.

"Grandpa!" yelled Sammy as he ran right up on his mother's heels. Melissa began to cry and James picked her up and held on to her.

Oh, dear God, he thought. *Please don't let this be happening.* He picked up his daughter and held her tight. His recently planted face hurt like the dickens.

Then, thankfully, the voice of Grandpa Luke, "Hey, James, Celeste, kids, over here!"

They found old Luke sitting on a pile of logs by the barn about 50 yards from the charred remains of the home where Celeste grew up.

"Oh, Daddy," cried Celeste as she hugged him tightly. James, Sammy, and Melissa joined in the hugging ceremony — a big Winstead family hug in the entrance of the old and weathered barn that somehow had managed to outlive the old farmhouse. No one could have

imagined that. Even now, the barn looked ready to give way at any second. Then again, it had looked that way ever since a young James Winstead first called on a pretty little girl named Celeste for the first time many years ago. Luke had lectured him on the fine art of treating his daughter with respect right on this very spot and James would have bet the farm (no pun intended) that the barn would surely collapse before he drove her home that night ("by ten o'clock boy, or I'll feed you to the pigs!").

As the tears dried and the realization that Luke was all right began to settle into their minds and hearts, the obvious questions began to fly around the frigid night air, all aimed in Grandpa's general direction. These questions, though, all boiled down to *what happened?*

"In a nutshell, my Christmas lights burned it down!" said Grandpa Luke. "I should have been more careful I guess."

He hung his head and just shook it back and forth.

"Those old strands of lights were old and decrepit, just like me. I strung them all around the place and BOOM! A spark here, a spark there and stuff just started going up. I called the fire department, grabbed a jacket and a warm blanket and left. I sat here by the barn and watched it all burn. I should have known better."

"Thank God that you are okay, Dad!" cried Celeste. "What about all the stuff?"

"Hey, my sweet daughter, it's just stuff," said Luke.

"But," Celeste protested, "all of Mom's things! Pictures, everything. . . . Oh, Daddy."

"Sweet Pea, insurance money will build another house and all of that stuff is not needed for me to remember your mother.

"I see her face every night in my dreams. She is in heaven now and someday I will join her there on that beautiful shore. That is really all that matters. Had not God seen fit to save me tonight, I would be with her right now. By the way, merry Christmas."

"What happens now?" asked Sammy.

"I'm cold," shivered Melissa.

Luke picked his granddaughter up in his arms and held her real tight. "Y'all get back home now, I'll be just fine here in the barn. I have an old heater and —"

"We won't hear of that!" exclaimed James. "We are not leaving you, Lucas. Let's get in the Cherokee and head back for home. You can live with us until we get this new house built."

"I can't leave this farm!" cried Luke. "Who will look after my animals? I could never stand to leave them here. I won't leave them here!"

"We can take them with us, too," said Melissa.

"Great idea," said Grandpa. "James, go around the other side of the barn and get that old trailer. We can hook it up to the Cherokee and —"

"Ho there," cried out James. "What are we talking about here? How many? We can't take —"

"How many, Grandpa?" asked the voice of NASCAR.

"Well, there is Bess of course and other than that, just the pig, the lamb, and the rooster. That's all. Never got another dog after Bluey died and the cats all ran off when the weather turned cold. They'll fit in the trailer easily."

It was well after 4 a.m. when the Winstead Jeep Cherokee returned home to Sandy Cove. Grandpa sat in the back seat with Sammy and Melissa and sang Christmas songs to them as they nodded off. His old banjo had burned up in the fire or else he would have been pickin' as well as singin'. James saw this as somewhat of a positive. The rusty old horse trailer that was attached to the SUV carried one cow, one lamb, one pig, and a cantankerous banty rooster.

Everyone who abided in the neighborhood of Sandy Cove was fast asleep. Each house was shrouded in darkness waiting for Christmas Day to arrive.

The street was just as quiet as a mouse on silk. Rudolph and the other reindeer stood there silhouetted in the cold darkness of the Winstead front lawn.

The Wal-Mart supercenter had closed long ago and was locked up tight. There would be no presents and no turkey dinner for the Winsteads this year. James would tie Bess up behind the house and perhaps put the pig in the garage. The lamb could stay in the downstairs bathroom and they would put the rooster in the utility room. The couch in the den pulled out and could be made into somewhat of a bed for Lucas. What a night!

A short while later the sun began to rise over the tiny subdivision of Sandy Cove. The Winstead family was in a deep sleep. James and Celeste held each other tightly beneath the covers of their queen-size bed.

Melissa was snuggled up tightly in her bed. She was fast asleep in her Barbie pajamas and dreaming of Santa Claus. Samuel was deep within the "pit area," dreaming

of Talladega. Grandpa was on the pullout sofa dreaming of his dear departed wife.

Then, deep within the utility room, from just about one foot in front of the Kenmore washing machine and dryer rose up the loudest and most hideous sound that the good people of Sandy Cove had ever heard. The screeching sound of Luke's rooster literally tingled the spine.

At least the police didn't show up. Several calls from frightened neighbors and a few shaky nerves were the only result of the rooster's unearthly squeal.

Melissa stood at the foot of her parents' bed holding onto her favorite teddy bear.

"I thought a rooster was supposed to go 'cock-a-doo-dle-dooooo,'" she said softly.

"Well, obviously, this one doesn't," answered a very weary James Winstead. "Go back to bed now, Peanut. Grandpa has it all taken care of."

Actually, Grandpa Luke just banged on the utility room door and yelled, "Shut up, the sun doesn't shine in there."

He was now back on the couch, fast asleep.

"What about Santa?" Melissa asked.

"We'll talk about it later, Honey," answered Celeste. "Go back to bed for awhile."

James continued to lay there wide-awake for about an hour. He stared at the ceiling and tried to sort all of this out; however, the events of the last 24 hours seemed way beyond his comprehension.

"James," whispered Celeste. "You okay?"

"Yeah, I'm all right, Honey. It's just that this whole thing is, well, unfortunate to say the least." He sighed.

"Well, it's inconvenient for sure, but with God's help, we'll get through it, as a family. Merry Christmas, Baby." She kissed him on the cheek.

It was around 11 a.m. on Christmas morning when Celeste, James, Samuel, and Melissa finally woke up. They all came downstairs and found Grandpa Lucas on the telephone. He had already lit up the tree and was talking to an old friend and neighbor named Jeff Douglas.

Old farmer Douglas owned a ninety-acre spread of land about half way between Sandy Cove and Grandpa's farm. Luke was talking on the telephone as the Winsteads entered the living room.

"Okay, great! Bye-bye, Jeff. Merry Christmas! Thanks! Talk to you soon."

He hung up the phone and stood up.

"Well now, merry Christmas, gang! Come over here and hug your ol' Grandpa Luke."

Melissa and Sammy ran full speed into his outstretched arms and nearly knocked the old man over.

"Merry inconvenient Christmas, Grandpa!" shouted Melissa.

James made some coffee while Celeste rattled through the pots and pans and the cupboard. She thought that some canned soup with a few personal touches might be in order. She found some herbs and spices that she had seen used on the "Cooking with Emeril" show on the Food-TV channel and went to work.

In the Winstead living room there was a big burgundy-colored couch that faced two semi-matching chairs. There was a low-sitting marble floor piece that sat between that acted as a table or a catch all of sorts. Behind the chairs was a bookcase. Just to the side of where they were all sitting was a beautiful eight-foot-high blue spruce Christmas tree. It was adorned with several hundred blinking colored lights and a plethora of decorations ranging from little dangling Santas, to balls of all shapes and sizes. But mostly, there were singing and praying angels.

Celeste collected angelic Christmas ornaments and each year there were more on the family tree than the year before. At the very top of the tree there stood a great angel in shimmering white with his arms outstretched to the heavens and at the foot of the tree rested a beautiful manger scene backlit by a white bulb.

What was missing of course, were presents. *Thanks to Shopazon-dot-com*, thought James as he sipped his Starbucks Sumatra coffee. He felt that he had really dropped the ball on this strange Christmas, and the sight of his children sitting here with no presents to open was almost more than a daddy could bear.

The family sat in the semi-circle of the living room quietly eating a bowl of some of Celeste's famous turkey giblet soup, courtesy of Campbell's and Emeril.

Grandpa spoke first.

"Jeff Douglas is coming over later this afternoon to take Bess and the other animals to his farm," he said very matter-of-factly as if this sort of thing happened every day. "He also said that I could live in his little guest house while they rebuild my place."

He sat his soup bowl down and picked up his coffee cup.

"You can stay here, Dad. You know that," said Celeste.

"Much appreciated. But his farm is closer, and I can oversee things better from there."

Grandpa Luke put his cup down and started back in on the soup.

"Oh, please leave the rooster," laughed Samuel and everyone joined in laughing. Sammy was, indeed, a very funny kid!

"That thing is horrible," said Melissa. "He probably scared off Santa."

They continued to eat their soup in silence.

No turkey dinner today, thought Celeste. There just wasn't time!

I'll never shop on the Internet again! Some father I am, thought James.

No presents, no nothing! thought little Melissa.

This Christmas stinks. I'll bet Michael Waltrip is having a HUGE Christmas! thought Sammy.

Grandpa Luke broke the silence and interrupted the Winstead family's thought process.

"Melissa, what did you say when you greeted your ol' Grandpa this morning?" he asked.

"I said 'Merry inconvenient Christmas,' Grandpa," she whispered softly. "Sammy called it that last night."

"Inconvenient Christmas, huh, Sam?" he looked in the boy's direction.

"Well, duh. Yeah, look around. What a night! What a day! Everything just went whack-o this year, Grandpa. A real pile-up in the third turn, if you ask me. Luckily no one was injured in this crash."

More giggles from Melissa.

"Tell you what, kiddos. Help your mother pick up these dishes and all of you come and gather around this here beautiful tree. I have a story to tell you. You all seem to have a little case of what my dear, departed saint of a wife would call the 'mully-grubs.' You think this is inconvenient. Well, I'll admit, it certainly is a bit unfortunate. However, I want to tell you all about the most inconvenient Christmas that ever was."

The family gathered around Grandpa Luke. James and Sam grabbed chairs, while Celeste and Melissa sat in the twinkling glow of tree lights. Their grandfather now had their full attention.

Luke began to tell his story.

"About two thousand years ago, in a very far-away land there lived a beautiful young lady named Mary who had fallen deeply in love with a carpenter by the name of Joseph. They were to marry."

"Grandpa," moaned Melissa, "is this the story of Baby Jesus? I know this story!"

Sammy chimed right in. "We learned about this stuff in Sunday school when we were little!"

"I see," said Grandpa Luke. "But, please, allow me to tell you all about it just one more time. You may not have ever heard the whole story before."

"Okay, Grandpa, shoot the works," laughed

Melissa. That was another one of Daddy's sayings and it caused Celeste and James to smile.

"But if it gets boring, Grandpa, I am waving the yellow flag on ya," said Sammy with conviction.

"I promise not to bore you," said Lucas in a matter-of-fact tone of voice, although he couldn't hide the little twinkle in his eye. He dearly loved these children. He could see his dearly departed Emma in their every move. James and his daughter Celeste were good parents and he was proud of them. This had been a terrible Christmas for all of them, but perhaps his little story could bring them all some holiday cheer and even more importantly, bless their hearts and bring them closer to God.

"Mary was happy, thinking about their future together. She was alone in her room when all of a sudden, a great angel from heaven stood before her. He appeared to be bathed in a white light."

"Like on 'Touched By An Angel' on television?" asked Melissa.

"Well, sort of like that I guess, but much bigger and brighter than the angels on TV," said Grandpa. "Anyhow, it had to have scared poor little Mary half to death. This wasn't just any angel either. It was one of God's main helpers— an angel by the name of Gabriel."

"Whoa!" whispered Sammy.

"Gabriel told Mary that she was blessed among women. He told her that she would have a child and that she would name him Jesus and that God himself was the father. Just like that, she was pregnant. Now came the hard part. She had to tell Joseph that she was going to have this special baby and that *he* would *not* be the father. She shared the story with him. He wasn't mad or anything because he loved her so very much that he just had to believe her. Well, it turns out that God rewarded Joseph's faith by sending an angel to visit him as well.

"This angel backed up the whole incredible story and certainly put Joseph's mind at ease. This was his first time to ever talk to an angel as well and it had to be pretty freaky."

"Totally freaky," sighed Sammy.

"To the MAX!" agreed Melissa.

"About nine months later, Mary was really pregnant when all of a sudden Joseph had a tax problem!"

"Huh?" asked James. "I never heard about that part. A tax problem? Even back then?"

Celeste couldn't help but laugh at her husband's outburst.

"There was a great Caesar in Rome back then named Augustus who decreed that all the world should be taxed!" continued Grandpa Luke. "You see, the Romans ruled just about everything and whatever Caesar wanted, Caesar received and he was wanting more money for the government coffers."

"Sounds familiar," grumbled James.

"It gets worse. There was a catch. Every citizen would have to go back to his own hometown to pay this tax. Now, Joseph and Mary were living in Galilee, in the village of Nazareth, and Joseph had been born about a hundred miles or so away in the town of Bethlehem, which was in Judea."

"That was a little town, right?" laughed Celeste. She finally got in a good one.

"Yes, it was, sweet daughter," answered Lucas. "The little town of Bethlehem."

"You know people didn't have very good transportation in those days. Most of the time they just walked. This presented a real problem for Joseph, for his wife was now very heavy with child. So, he bought a little donkey to carry Mary and they walked all the way to Bethlehem. They arrived in town and had to be so tired. In fact, Mary knew that the birth of the baby was very close.

" 'Joseph, you better get us a room and I mean quick' is what she probably said.

"Well, the little town of Bethlehem was just

hustling and bustling. People were just everywhere. Joseph tried so hard to find a room for the night. He checked several boarding houses and inns and they all turned him away."

"No room at the Holiday Inn," said Samuel. "Must have been a big race in town!"

"The Ramada and the Hilton were filled up as well!" laughed Grandpa. "Joseph begged and pleaded well into the night until finally, an innkeeper showed some mercy. 'Look,' he said. 'I have an old lean-to stable. Take your wife on back there and feel free to spend the night. There is some livestock, but just ignore them. You can make a bed on the hay.' "

Just then Bess the cow let out a huge "moo" sound from the Winstead backyard.

"I think we can relate," laughed Celeste.

Luke continued, "So, as Joseph and Mary made a place for themselves in the stable some very magical events were taking place elsewhere. Angels began to appear to shepherds. These guys are out in the fields all bleary-eyed and tired and BOOM! All of a sudden the sky is just full of angels singing and rejoicing and shouting the message that the Messiah who had been foretold by all the prophets of old would be born this night in a manger. How convincing that must have been — a sky full of angels."

"Shut right on up!" cried out Melissa. "*Cool!*"

"Melissa," said Celeste as she frowned at her daughter, "don't you dare tell your Grandpa to shut up."

"Oh no, Mom," explained Sammy. "*Shut up* doesn't really mean *shut up*; it means *wow*."

James rolled his eyes toward the ceiling and said, "Well, *shut up* and I mean *shut up* as in *shut up* and let your Grandpa Luke finish his story."

"Well, the shepherds heeded the words of the angels and started to make a beeline for Bethlehem. Meanwhile a terrible thing was happening. There was a king appointed by the Roman caesar to rule over this part of the kingdom and he was not a nice guy at all. His name was Herod the Great, although he wasn't really all that great. Well, he had heard a rumor that there were wise men from a far-away land that had been following a star in the heavens. These three kings believed that this star would lead them to a newly born king — the new Messiah, whose birth would signify a new message of peace and love for all of mankind. Scholars had been waiting for this birth for a long time and here lately, with the appearance of angels and a new star moving across the sky, it seemed that the prophecies of old were beginning to come true. None of this pleased Herod.

"He sent word to these three that he wanted a meeting with them and he wanted it now! So, they came before Herod. Herod wanted to know about this star. When did it first appear? He just couldn't stand the thought of a new king being born right there under his very nose. He was feeling very challenged in his power.

The king ordered them to report back."

"That's awful, Grandpa," said Sammy. "Did they rat Jesus out?"

"No way! Here is how it happened. Jesus was born on that first Christmas Day. Mary wrapped Him in swaddling clothes — that's strips of cloth to you and me — and laid Him down in a bed of hay in a manger. Even the animals bowed their heads when He was born. The shepherds who had heard the angels sing all showed up to kneel and pray and thank God for sending His Son to save mankind. There they were — Joseph and Mary, some barn animals and a handful of lowly shepherds. And there before them was God's only Son who would someday die on a Cross so that we may all have eternal life. As if this wasn't enough, the sky once again filled with angels singing songs with a lyric of 'Glory to God in the highest, peace on Earth and good will toward men.' It had to have really been a moment.

"But the kings didn't rat Jesus out. God warned them in a dream and told them not to go back to

Herod but to pretty much skedaddle back to where they came from and they did just that. But you just can't keep an event like that very low-key, so the word did get back to Herod about the birth of the new King. He decided then to send troops into all of the surrounding lands and kill every newborn son. He figured in so doing, he would surely put an end to this problem! I told you he was not very nice."

"How did they escape, Grandpa?" asked Melissa. Her eyes were as big as saucers.

"Once again, an angel came to the rescue. It could have even been Gabriel. He told Joseph to take Mary and the Child out of Bethlehem right away. He said that Joseph should flee under the cover of darkness to the land of Egypt and stay there until the angel came to him again and told him it was safe to return. So, Joseph loaded Mary and Baby Jesus back onto the donkey and they hit the road. A very inconvenient Christmas, if you ask me." Grandpa sat back and smiled. "Inconvenient, indeed."

"Right!" Sammy smiled. "A young girl with a child she can't explain is forced to walk a hundred miles just to give birth in the hay while the evil king, feeling all threatened in his power, sends his troops to hunt them down and wipe them out!"

"Yup, hands-down, kids," answered Grandpa "that had to be the most inconvenient Christmas that ever was. That was also the night that God came so far to give himself to all of us through the birth of His only Son, Jesus Christ."

Celeste, wiping a tear, rose up from her seat and disappeared down the hall. She returned with four beautifully wrapped presents and handed one out to each of them. "Those packages that came the other day?" she began. "Well, they weren't *just* pillow shams and new bedding. There was some other stuff in there, as well." She couldn't help but smile. She had pulled off a good one and her timing couldn't have been any better. Everyone was so surprised.

"Presents!" squealed Melissa. "Oh, thank you, Mommy!"

Melissa opened her present first, a big square box that contained a wonderful purple-colored Sony combination radio, cassette and CD player with little pink headphones. "Wow! Thanks, Mom! My favorite color! How very cool." She looked at Sammy. "I have my own player now, you turkey!"

Her big brother responded with his favorite monster face as he picked up his own surprise box, which really wasn't very big.

Sammy carefully removed the NASCAR wrapping paper from his gift as he looked up. "Nice touch, Mom," he smiled. The package was relatively light as well.

He opened up the box and pulled out a checkered

flag — *a real one!* In one corner, there was a huge signature written with a black Sharpie — "Michael Waltrip #15."

"Ahhhhhhhhhhhhhh," Sammy squealed as he hugged his mom. "Unbelieeeeevvable!"

"You know that race he won in Daytona last year? That was the very flag that ended the race. I got it on Ebay," she said.

Celeste had known that the flag would be a huge hit and it was. Little Samuel was nearly in tears. *Maybe he'll clean his room for me now,* she thought. *Nah!*

James was next. He opened up a pretty good-sized box, reached inside and pulled out a navy-colored heavy-duty and most assuredly, "very toasty" parka. He stood up and put it on. "Wow, um, thanks, Hon," he said as pulled the hood up over his head looking like Nanook of the North.

"I have one just like it," said Celeste.

"Matching parka coats? Is there a good 'why' for this?"

"Look in the inside pocket," she said.

James pulled out two airplane tickets and before he could even look at them Celeste hollered. "In February, we are going to *Alaska*! Merry Christmas!"

James was stricken. Ever since their first date he had talked about going to Alaska someday and over the past few years he and Celeste had just become so busy working and raising up kids, that he had just put it out of his mind. "This is great!" he said and grabbed his wife up in his arms and hugged her tight. "*Alaska . . . wow!*"

Grandpa sat and smiled. He was still holding on to his square-shaped box, which was all wrapped up in green and yellow John Deere tractor paper.

"Your turn, Dad," whispered Celeste.

He opened his present and began to weep. He just couldn't help it. In his two weathered hands he was now holding a beautifully framed black-and-white picture of him and his Emma sitting on the old front porch of the now burned-to-the-ground farmhouse. She was smiling and looking up at him with her left arm around his waist and he was mugging for the camera. *Being silly,* he thought. They couldn't have been more than 25 years old. Celeste sat beside him and laid her head on his shoulder.

"Mom gave me that picture a long time ago, Dad. I have always meant to frame it and give it to you. I'm not sure what took me so long. Perhaps, the time was right today."

Lucas wiped away another tear and took his daughter into his arms as if she was still a little girl. "I love you, my dear one. When I see you and these two kids, I see her. Thank you for a wonderful Christmas."

Just then a heavy knock came on the front door. It was Jeff Douglas.

"Hello, everyone. Merry Christmas. I'm here to pick up the critters," he laughed. "I already hooked up your trailer, Lucas, and Bess is already aboard."

While Grandpa Luke and James were rounding up the pig and the lamb and that awful rooster, another car pulled up into the drive. It was Dave and Margie Boots from Your Town Truck Stop. They were carrying some huge pans that contained a cooked and fully dressed turkey as well as two homemade casseroles.

"Hey, there," said Dave. Celeste could see that the front license plate on his big Dodge pickup read "Call me Bub!" "We got word about the fire last night and we put two and two together pretty quick. Margie thought you guys could use a little home cooking on this Christmas Day."

"We just need to fire it up a little and we'll all be ready to eat. Merry Christmas," said Margie as she made her way right into the kitchen.

A bit later on, they were stuffed with turkey and trimmings.

"I think a prayer is in order," said James and everyone stood and took each other by the hand. They stood before God as one, in a small circle.

Dear precious and Heavenly Father, we thank You on this Christmas Day for Your many blessings. You have taught us today that even when everything in our lives seems to be going wrong, You are still looking after us and blessing us with Your love and mercy. Continue to teach us Your will, Oh Lord, and may we always remember to put You first in our lives. Thank You for sending Your Son to us on that very inconvenient Christmas long ago. In Jesus' wonderful name, and everyone said?

"AMEN!" everyone cheered.

After dinner, their friends Ken and Jane Dye who lived next door came over, and while James was catching them up on the incredible events of the last 24 hours, Celeste made some hot chocolate. As Bub was pouring some into his cup, he turned to little Sammy and asked. "What was that your father called that first Christmas long ago? Inconvenient?"

"Oh, yes," said Sammy in his best NASCAR announcer's voice. "We have learned today, race fans, that by far and away, yes, hands down! The most inconvenient Christmas that ever was — was the first!"

*M*erry Christmas to all and may God bless you and yours!

About the Songwriter

As a long-time lover of Christmas music, I'd be first to acknowledge that the world doesn't need another Christmas song trying to compete for attention. But the songwriter in me was always bothered by how few Christmas song lyrics related to my life in any way. They tended to be a celebration of the kind of perfect Christmas that exists only in our collective Norman Rockwell imaginations and not in the reality in which I live. A father of small children, I know how much work goes in to making Christmas happen and how rarely the thing goes off as planned!

Perfect Christmases are also downright un-biblical. The Bible sets the first Christmas in one of the darkest periods of human history. It is impossible for any of us in the modern Western world to imagine the depravity of the ancient world, the cruelty of the Roman occupation, a time before modern science — much less modern medicine — and before much sanitation, before indoor plumbing, before anything resembling the Bill of Rights, a time of public pagan rituals, temple prostitutes and child sacrifice, to say nothing of life within the brutally persecuted Jewish community.

The good news of Christmas is that Jesus was born precisely into such darkness and for its sake. And, this is a word I need to hear again every Christmas season. The biblical witness is that God's own inconvenient Christmas and the true meaning of Christmas are one and the same thing. God has gone out of His way so that we could be shown the way.

Those of us striving to make Christmas meaningful again and again each year will be forever disappointed until we begin to grasp the paradox God has set before us. We must lose Christmas to find it. We must mature to that childlike place where — rather than chaffing at the inconveniences — we, in the spirit of Christ, seek to inconvenience ourselves, and take what little light we have into the great darkness of our world.

–Kyle Matthews

Many thanks to The Oak Ridge Boys for bringing my song to life in the studio and on stage, and to Joe Bonsall in particular for listening so carefully and for acting on his inspiration. Thanks as well to my mentor Michael Puryear, to my publisher Marty Wheeler, and to John Oullette for their invaluable help in this project.

And thanks to my inspirations: Susan, Emily and Christopher

–Kyle Matthews

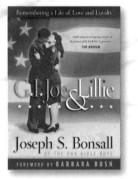